# FREE YOUR
# SPIRIT

POCKET EDITION

Published from
Mardukite Borsippa HQ, San Luis Valley, Colorado
Mardukite Academy & Systemology Society
*for spiritual or educational purposes only*

# FREE YOUR SPIRIT

Systemology
Professional Course
Booklet #5

Developed by Joshua Free
for the Systemology Society

© 2023, JOSHUA FREE

ISBN : 978-1-961509-29-0

Pocket Paperback Edition — *November 2023*

**mardukite.com**

# Learn How To Let Your Spirit Fly...
## Then Chart Your Flight For Ascension!

Unlock your ultimate spiritual potential by removing barriers to your true native state.

Learn how to easily attain Self-actualization and help to actualize others along the way.

A greater appreciation and understanding of *Spiritual Life* and *Existence* awaits you. Expand your reach to achieve your dreams.

Each 'Professional Course' lesson-booklet offers simple exercises and techniques that directly apply the philosophy of Systemology, assisting to increase your true knowingness, improve your capabilities in this life, and even decide what you will do in your next.

At the Mardukite Academy of Systemology, the 'Professional Course' lessons in this series are presented to Seeker's that have completed the 'Basic Course', previously released as six lesson-booklets, or the six-in-one single volume edition "Fundamentals of Systemology."

This all new presentation of the Systemology 'Pathway-to-Ascension' takes Seekers and continuing students from "Zero" to "Infinity" at lightning-fast speeds!

## Discover Who You Really Are...
## Because You Were Never Human

# TABLET OF CONTENTS

COURSE INTRODUCTION

LESSON FIVE:
FREE YOUR SPIRIT

APPENDIX

# PROFESSIONAL
# COURSE
# INTRODUCTION

## WELCOME, SEEKER!
## LET'S CHART YOUR JOURNEY
## ON THE PATHWAY

*Systemology* is a "holistic" approach to understanding the human experience. It is not actually a singular "subject" in itself, but rather, a new way in which to view the many subjects of *Life* and all *Existence*.

This is a professional course in *Systemology*—specifically, how to *apply* the spiritual philosophy of *Mardukite Systemology* as a personal *"Pathway"* to Ascension. Our *Systemology* is a new approach to *"Self-Actualization."* It is completely relevant for the modern age and the future; and quite different from any previous similar attempts, or other traditions, you might find. What's more: it is applicable to anyone with any background.

This *"Professional Course"* series of lessons (booklets) immediately follows the material given in the *"Basic Course"* series—available as six separate pocket-sized booklets, or in a single hardcover volume titled: *"Fundamentals of Systemology: A New Thought For The 21st Century."*

This is a *new* presentation of *Systemology*, emphasizing the application of our philosophy for those *Seekers* that are *"Flying-Solo"*—or else working through their studies and exercises as solitary practitioners. This is a new innovation for *Systemology*. Aside from the book *"Crystal Clear,"* all of our former advanced courses have placed a focus on *"Traditional Piloting"*—where experienced practitioners assist *Seekers* in *"processing."*

To receive the greatest benefit from this study: it is expected that a *Seeker* will already be familiar with the fundamental concepts and terminology (previously relayed in the *Basic Course*) before using lessons from the *Professional Course*. This will allow us to cover the extensive territory of the *Pathway* much more quickly. However, for reference, a basic *"glossary"* of vocabulary used in this lesson is provided in the *"appendix."*

## A NEW VIEW OF THE HUMAN SPIRIT

*Systemology* is not a religion and does not require any type of *faith*. It is, however, built upon a "spiritual" premise—and as such is an "applied spiritual philosophy." It is based on ancient teachings that we are *Spiritual Beings* essentially "wearing" bodies like clothes—or using them as "vehicles." Yet our true native nature is not *physical*, but beyond this existence; and we can certainly operate a "body" from *outside* of it.

We are **all** *Spiritual Beings*—each of us a *unit* of *Spiritual Awareness*—that have experienced a very long *Spiritual Timeline* of existence. Although we might be particularly attached to the familiar "physical shells" associated with *this* lifetime, our true *"Spiritual Lifetime"* is seemingly *eternal*. We have been many things before *Human*, and we go onward as a *Spiritual Being* after our *"genetic vehicle"* of *this* incarnation perishes.

While a "spiritual" view of the *Human Condition* may not seem unique to our philosophy, just how often is the concept treated *systematically*? For that matter: just how many people, supposedly raised to this or that religion, or professing to believe one thing or another, actually live their lives as though they are *Spirits*?

As *Spiritual Beings* of immortal existence and infinite potential, we are not simply the *"creations"* of an even greater *Being-*

*ness*; we are, in fact, an integral part of that *"creative force"* which permeates all existence.

Our basic nature is to be a *"creative being"*—our highest goals are *"to create."* And as such a being—which we refer to as an *Alpha-Spirit* in *Systemology*—we have run into some difficulties along the course of our *Spiritual Timeline* and found ourselves trapped within material *Universes* of our own collaborative *creation.*

Since we did not start out our existence in a trapped condition, it is correct to say that we have *"fallen"* from our native *"godlike"* states. It did not happen all at one, but progressively and systematically. We know our "troubles" have resulted from accumulated "barriers" and "blockages"—or *fragmentation*—during our vast experiences as *Spiritual Beings.* They are not because we lack something; but because of what's been added.

15

In *Systemology*, we systematically examine those routes by which we must have descended to reach our present condition, then reverse the direction of travel and chart a personal *"Pathway to Ascension."* Of course, the exact "details" of the *Spiritual Timeline* will be different for each individual *Seeker*. However, we have been able to systematically chart our *Pathway* based on common patterns of *Human fragmentation*.

In the most basic terms: the *fragmentation* that defines our "downward spiral" consists of decisions or considerations where we deny our true nature. This includes those decisions to *"withdraw"* rather than *"reach"*; where we choose to *not-know* rather than *know*; to *not-communicate* rather than *communicate*; and ultimately, to take *no-responsibility* for being a *creative-cause*, and therefore succumb to being an *effect*.

But there is *hope!* And much more importantly: there is an effectively workable *way out* of the mazes and traps of our existence. If you are reading this now, you have already begun to gather your tools and build up the *"horsepower"* necessary to break the gravity holding your *Spiritual Beingness* to the *Human Condition*.

---

## STUDYING THE PROFESSIONAL COURSE

Most *Seekers* study and practice *Systemology* at-a-distance and independent of the "Mardukite Academy" or any "Master-level" mentors trained therein. This means that the *books* (and to a lesser degree, the *internet*) are the only means of direct contact a *Seeker* maintains with the "Systemology Society" during their studies. A continuing *Seeker* from the "*Basic Course*" will be familiar with the style of study found in *this* course.

Misunderstood words are the most common reason an individual abandons studying a subject. When a misunderstanding occurs, *Awareness* declines. These misunderstandings start to "stack up" after the first occurrence, and as a result, the level of interest and attention will also decline. This is how a "confusion" develops; and the individual will get "bored" with the subject, feel tired, and unable to concentrate.

One solution is to return to the part of the material that was still interesting and enjoyable to read. When scanning around that area of text, there is likely to be a new word (or new specific use of a familiar word) that is unclear, but was passed by unnoticed. All *Systemology* books include their own *glossary*. Using this *glossary* and a high-quality dictionary will help resolve this misunderstanding once it is located.

An effective education of any subject is taught on a *gradient*. This is what is intended by presenting the study of something as "*grades*." Rather than treating a subject as one total mass, true learning is achieved by increasing one's understanding with a *gradual* increase upward. The *ascent* to a mountaintop is not successfully achieved in one leap, but by targeting and reaching specific checkpoints along the way.

This *Professional Course* consists of a series of lessons (booklets) that gradually increase a *Seeker's* ability to understand and apply the practices and techniques of *Systemology* as a complete "*Pathway to Ascension*." It is an appropriate study for continuing *Seekers* (from the *Basic Course*), but also "advanced" *Systemologists*.

Each lesson (booklet) of the *Professional Course* applies *Systemology* to a particular subject (or focus). It is best if the entire course can be studied and applied in sequential order. These lessons also employ a style of practice or technique called *"Systematic Processing."* An introduction to applying this methodology is provided in the final lesson (booklet) of the *Basic Course*—or in the *"Fundamentals of Systemology"* volume.

To study the *Professional Course* just like a student at the Academy: a *Seeker* reads through all instructional material and applies each exercise (or *"process"*) presented in the text to the extent they comfortably can, before continuing on to the next lesson (booklet).

When first starting on the *Pathway* as a *Solo* practitioner, without the aid of an experienced *Pilot*, a *Seeker* shouldn't "push too hard" or allow themselves to get too "stuck" on any one area (lesson) or *process*. It is not expected that any one area will be completely handled when first introduced. For optimum results, it is expected that a serious *Seeker* will make more than one "pass" through the entire *Professional Course*.

The *Professional Course* is not altogether different from other forms of practical or technical education: where the instruction and exercises are delivered to a completion, and then a student further increases their abilities, strength and skill-level by applying additional practice throughout their life. Therefore, a student should not concern themselves with perfectly mastering each step (or lesson) before progressing forward.

Additional passes through the material are likely to result in different "*realizations*" (an increased *level of understanding*) than a previous time. New "layers" of *Knowingness* may now be accessible during a *process* that may not have been before. It is important to avoid invalidating the progress you've made just because one area is not completely handled right away, or if a certain *process* seems too difficult on the first pass.

## CHARTING A COURSE ON
## THE PATHWAY

Although we can communicate a systematic structure to *fragmentation,* the personal journey experienced along the *Pathway* will be different for each *Seeker.* For example, certain areas will seem more *"turbulent"* or difficult for one *Seeker* than another. We tend to say that these areas have more *"charge"* on them—or that they are more *"heavily charged."* It is best to handle such areas when you are already feeling "good" and not in a situation (or condition) where that specific area is consistently being *"triggered"* or *"restimulated."*

As an applied philosophy, *Systemology* "theory" can be easily utilized in the "laboratory" of the "world-at-large" in everyday life. This is implied within the basic instruction of each lesson. Unlike other "sciences" that conduct experiments by making a change to some "objective variable" *out there* and waiting to see an effect, our focus is the individual (or *Observer*) themselves, and how *they* affect the "*Reality*" perceived.

In addition to applying *Systemology* "New Thought" to everyday life, our philosophy is applied by using specific exercises and systematic techniques. These "*processes*" provide the most stable personal gain (and *realizations*) for each area; but only when actually applied with a *Seeker's* full "*presence*" and *Awareness*.

This *Professional Course* is designed so that it may be easily read and studied with little concern for what "dangers" these teachings—or *processing*—might unleash. However, there are still some guidelines that pertain to the "best-uses" of these course lessons, particularly if a *Seeker* intends for stable development.

Skipping over too much material/*processing* in early lessons may make attempts to understand (or apply) later lessons more difficult. However, once the complete *Professional Course* is worked through at least once in its entirety, specific areas can then be later returned to and treated with a greater sense of *Awareness* and *"presence"* than before. Of course, in *"Traditional Piloting,"* the rate of processing is monitored by an experienced practitioner; but in *"Solo-Processing,"* a *Seeker* must regulate their own progress on the *Pathway*.

Applying a systematic technique is called *"running a process."* The *processes* are designed with very simple instructions or "*command-lines*." To *run* a *processing command-line*, a *Seeker* may be assisted by the communication of that *line* from a "*Co-Pilot*" (as in "*Traditional Piloting*"). But even then, a *Seeker* must still personally "input" the *command* as *Self*. For this reason —and quite thankfully— *Solo-Processing* is possible.

---

## TAKING FLIGHT ON THE PATHWAY

*Processing Techniques* are intended to treat the *Spiritual Being* or *Alpha-Spirit*; the individual themselves. It is applied by the *Alpha-Spirit*—then *Self-directed* to the "Mind-System" or even a "body" (*genetic-vehicle*), both of which are "constructs" that the *Alpha-Spirit* (*Self*, or the "I-AM" *Awareness unit*) operates, but neither of which is actually *Self*. *Fragmentation* causes *Humans* to falsely identify *Self as* the "*Mind*" or even a "*Body*."

The *Professional Course* lessons (booklets) are designed for the *Beginning Seeker* in mind—one that may have an understanding of theory, but with little experience in practice. That being said: each of these lessons may be used toward total *Beta-Defragmentation* within a specific area. There are also more *processes* given for each subject than may be necessary to achieve an *ultimate end-point realization* on that entire area.

Some *processes* can be treated quite lightly at first; others may require a bit of working at in order to get *"running"* well. It is important to set aside a period of time when you can be dedicated to your studies and *processing*. This period of time is referred to as a *"processing session."* The reason for this, is that when a *process* does start *running* well, it is important to be able to complete it to a satisfactory *"end-point."*

The purpose of *systematic processing* is to be able to *really* "look" at things and even determine the *considerations* we have made—or attitudes we have decided— about *Reality* as a result of those experiences. It doesn't do us much good to simply "glance"—or to *restimulate* something uncomfortable and then quickly *withdraw* from it once again, leaving more of our *attention* yet again behind and held fixedly on it.

Generally speaking, a *Seeker* continues to *run* a *process* so long as something is "happening"—which is to say, the *process* is still producing a change. Usually this is evident by the type of "answers" that a *command-line* helps a *Seeker* originate from the database of their own *Mind-System*. The *command-lines* do not "do" anything on their own. They assist a *Seeker* to direct their own attention toward increasing *Awareness*.

Of course, a *Seeker* may also cease to generate new "data" from a *process* without reaching an *"ultimate"* realization as an *"end-point."* It is possible that additional "layers" (or even other "areas") require handling before anything "deeper" is accessible. If this is the case, end the *process*. But, if a *Seeker* is *withdrawing* from something uncomfortable that was incited or stirred up, then a *process* is *run* until they feel "good" about it.

In case the thought of encountering *"turbulence"* is a concern: the techniques given as *"Opening Procedures"* of a *Formal Session* (in the *Basic Course*), and those found in the earliest lessons of the *Professional Course*, are quite useful when applied as "safety nets" for maintaining *Awareness* and *presence*, even when *Flying-Solo*.

One of the benefits to *Flying-Solo* is that *processing* is entirely *Self-determined*. This already provides a certain built-in "safety" for a practitioner. Anything you *restimulate* by *Self-determinism* is *your thing*. It is not incited by external *other-determined* influences (or other "source-points" in existence) that make you an *effect*. It can be more easily handled in *processing*—or you can simply let things "cool down" and come back to it again.

While it may seem "mysterious" to beginners, a *Seeker* gets a sense for knowing how long to *run* a *process* only with practice. Once you have spent some time actually applying the *Professional Course*, there are many aspects that become "second nature" because they are, in fact, a part of our true original nature. All we have done is *"reverse engineer"* the routes of *creation* and *consideration* that are already *our own*.

# LESSON FIVE:
# FREE
# YOUR SPIRIT

## RELEASING THE SPIRIT

The previous lesson (booklet) for this *Professional Course* series emphasized *"Handling Humanity"* — or else the *processing* of *Human Problems*. These areas included *"protest," "change,"* and even the subject of *"help."* It is important to handle these *"surface areas"* that seem to more visibly *"press upon"* or *"interfere"* in the daily experience of life, before setting our sights on higher vistas — such as we will approach in *this* lesson.

To begin this lesson, we will focus more directly on treating the *Seeker* (or *Self*) *as* an *Alpha-Spirit*. This is always the intention — because it is the actual *Self* or *I-AM-Awareness* as an *Alpha-Spirit* that we are treating with *Systematic Processing;* not a *"Body"* or even a *"Mind."*

It is the *Spirit* that we direct our *"process-*

*ing command-lines"* ("PCL") to when applying our philosophy as exercises or techniques. It is *Self* that processes the command, then either performs the action or directs that command to a *"Mind"* or *"Body"* if it is called for. Both the *"Mind"* and *"Body"* are *constructs*; *Self* is *Eternal*.

*"Releasing the Spirit"* is a continuous goal as a *Seeker* progresses further on the *Pathway-to-Ascension*, and it is composed of many parts. It is not necessarily a "practice" or "technique"—or even a single area—in itself. We are continuously interested in "freeing" the *Spirit* from the trappings of a material existence.

On the one hand, we have the *considerations* of *Beingness* that an individual experiences for themselves as an *Alpha-Spirit* (or in many cases, as restricted to the *Human Condition*); on the other, we have the accumulated *fragmentation* that heavily "weighs" on the *Spirit*, and of which they are *compulsively creating* as "chains" that bind their *considerations* to lower-levels of material *Beingness* (*e.g.* the *Human Condition*).

It is a *cycle*. And in this lesson—as we start *"Systemology Level-2"*—we will explore and *process* each side of this reoccurring *cycle* directly.

---

## SPIRITUAL BEINGNESS

In our basic state—back behind all the circuitry of *"Mind-Systems"* and *"Bodies"*—we are a single unit of *Spiritual Awareness* (or *"ZU"*). In the past, philosophers that have come close to a true understanding have associated this true *"Spiritual Self"* as "pure thought."

To say that we are *"thought"* and that everything is *"Mind"* is only a part-of-the-way-there kind of truth. It at least demonstrates an understanding that *Self* is not a *"Body."* For some, this itself is milestones ahead of identifying exclusively with a *"Body"*; or certain *body parts* used to *"think"* with (as the expression goes).

The *Alpha-Spirit* is not composed of physical matter or energy; nor is it dependent on it for its own existence. In actuality, we are an *Awareness* with the ability to generate and observe *thought*. We also have the ability to *create energy* without requiring an "outside" *source*. A full *Knowingness* of all this is what we seek to reclaim ultimately with our *Ascension*.

There are spiritual philosophies and metaphysical traditions teaching about various *"astral"* and *"subtle"* *bodies* that also enshroud the *Alpha-Spirit*. These do exist—and we presume that they are metaphysical constructs used by the *Alpha-Spirit* in former *Universes*, or less "physically solid" (less condensed) versions of *Beta Existence*. However, none of these are the true "pure" *Spirit* either.

In our native state, we are not located, or even locatable, in "space-time"—because our existence *precedes* the *creation* of *Universes* to be located in. The idea of *Self* being "located" in a specific spot is really a matter of *reality-agreements* for the practical purposes of, for example, participating in a "game" far more than a matter of "actual fact."

A *"Free-Spirit"* can locate its *Awareness* (as a "point-of-view") anywhere it chooses simply by *intention*. This means, when not "entrapped" by *fragmented considerations*, one should be able to be *in* the "*body*" or *out* of it, at will. One should also be able to freely *pervade* their own "*Mind*"-construct, and be in total control of it.

The traditional "*astral work*" that is found in contemporary "New Age" material differs greatly from the type of *"spirit vision"*—or *"ZU-Vision"*—that is sought with the practice of *Systemology*. Most *"astral"* work is still very much entangled in the *Mind*, even if *Awareness* is separated from a *body*. Our practices are directed at points of *Awareness* superior to all the various energy fields and subtle bodies.

*"ZU-Vision"* is treated more directly at higher levels of *Systemology* work—but there are many reasons why we introduce the concept earlier on the *Pathway*. Most importantly, it is a "phenomenon" that *may* be encountered early on the *Pathway*—especially during the practice of *"objective processing"* (as given in earlier lessons), particularly when one is practicing the "advanced mental versions" of those techniques.

The pure *Spiritual Awareness* or *Alpha-Spirit* is the actual YOU—your *Self*—and it is quite capable of directly *creating*, *operating* and *perceiving* independent and exterior to *any* "*Body.*" However, as beings entrapped by our *considerations* for *Beingness* within *this* "*Physical Universe,*" we are primarily dependent on an "*organic-body*" (or "*genetic-vehicle*") in order to relay to us the sensory information of this existence.

Unfortunately, without achieving a high state of *Knowingness* during one's lifetime —from which *Ascension* may be reached —as an *actualized* state of *Awareness*, the metaphorical "gravity" (or "pull") of the *material world* and accumulated *fragmentation* (kept in all these "subtle" *bodies*), "weighs" heavily on *Self*; and it will continue to linger about looking for another similar "*body.*" We do not automatically become *Free-Spirits* imminently at "death."

## "ZU-VISION" AND PROCESSING

There are some *systematic processes* that prompt a *Seeker* to place their *Awareness* "exterior to" a *body*. By this, we do not simply mean "place their *attention*" — but to literally *"Be"* outside of the *body*. In actual practice, we do not mean "taking flight on some out-of-body journey" — but a stable ability to "stand outside" the *Body-Mind* systems and continue to control their operation as something altogether separate from *Self*.

This may happen earlier on the *Pathway* while *processing*, although its direct handling is reserved for upper-level *"Advanced Techniques"* (*A.T.*) of *Systemology*. However, we take this up now to provide a *Seeker* some sense of familiarity in case the phenomenon begins to occur; and there are some fun *processes* to *run* on this even if it has not happened.

A *Seeker* might experience the phenomenon very "suddenly" without intending to. This is a natural part of some of the *objective processing* when *run* for long periods of time. Although there is no danger in it, the "suddenness" and "unexpectedness" of the occurrence can affect later attempts to do this *knowingly.*

It usually is not the "getting out" part that causes *fragmentation* in this area, but the sudden "snapping-back-in" to a *body* that results from being startled by the phenomenon, or if the *body* is disturbed in its physical environment. This can create a *turbulent charge* on the entire subject, which of course makes later applications more difficult.

In an ideal situation, the *Alpha-Spirit* is *defragmented* and can easily move "in" or "out" without any sensation of "impact"; however, when the phenomenon occurs unintentionally, or an individual "gets out" carrying a lot of their *fragmented en-*

*ergetic-masses* with them, the sense of "impact" *can* be uncomfortable.

Barriers that hinder the *Awareness* of this native state and ability of the *Alpha-Spirit* are broken down little by little with *systematic processing*. This means that a *Seeker* is likely to experience the sudden phenomenon of "*ZU-Vision*" (perhaps for the first time, *knowingly*) during a *processing session*. Having some sense of this ahead of time will ease any worries and prepare a *Seeker* to handle it, if and when it does occur naturally.

In these early practices, we are not concerned with actually pulling your "normal" *point-of-view* (or "POV") of *Self*—and all of its "mental machinery" and "energy bodies" *&tc.*—out from their "usual" positions. And this is not necessary at this juncture of the *Pathway*, for the *Alpha-Spirit* (not being actually locatable itself) has an ability to establish

42

more than one POV simultaneously, and in multiple locations.

A *viewpoint*—or *"point-of-view"*—is a "point" *from* which to "view," or else "operate" our *Awareness*. In basic terms, all you would need to do to *create* a *second* (or *alternative*) one is to decide on a *spot* (or *point*, if you prefer) and start operating as an *Awareness* from it. You may leave your previous ("normal") *Human* POV where it is for these early practices, and simply *add* an additional one.

The actual YOU—the *Self* or *Alpha-Spirit*—is always *present* (providing *presence*) wherever *attention* and *Awareness* is oriented or directed. So, *you* are never using a POV *"remote"* from *you*—but in this case, we mean a POV that is *remote* from the *body*. This is what makes common use of the term *"remote viewing"* misleading.

# LOCATIONAL "POV" PROCESSING

*Locational* or *"POV" Processing* first appeared in the *"Imaginomicon"* volume of the *Systemology Core*. This practice is inspired by mystical training techniques found in *Franz Bardon's* work (see *Basic Course, Lesson-5*). Therein, *"transference of consciousness"* is described—where an *initiate* practices imagining their POV "going inside" solid masses (objects) that are separate from the *body*.

However, the original methods all seem to emphasize *flow* in *one*-direction only: the "going in" part. We can improve this practice for our *systematic processing* by using alternation: "going in" and "going out"—with repetition and fluidity.

Early experiments by research-members of the *Systemology Society* demonstrated that, initially, the best results come from practicing with "large" masses—ones that a *Seeker* is already familiar with, but which are not present in the immediate vicinity. Our standard instruction at the *Mardukite Academy* is to use "a mountain" (one which the individual is not already sitting on, if that is the case).

In *Traditional Piloting*, a "Co-Pilot" is not likely to have an objective reality on the *Seeker's* experience—or see whether or not the actions are being carried out. To remedy this: a *Seeker* may sometimes say "*okay*" after completing an instruction— or if a bit of time has passed in silence, it is customary for a *Pilot* to inquire, "*did you?*" This inquiry should not relay a tone of skepticism, but simply to prompt additional communication.

These practices found in "*Systemology Level-2*" do *not* demand a *Seeker* to have already achieved the much higher-level goal of completely separating from the "normal" *compulsively created POV* of *Be-*

*ingness* "in a body." This *process* is practiced by *"imagining"* a *secondary viewpoint.* There is no reason to imagine some *"mental body"* (or any connected "cords" or "threads") in order to *create* or *visualize* "mental imagery."

A better understanding of a *secondary viewpoint* or *POV* is achieved by direct practice. The traditional *"Locational POV"* processing command-lines ("PCL") are:

A. *"Imagine being above (a mountain) looking down on it."*

B1. *"Imagine your viewpoint moving in to it."*

B2. *"Imagine your viewpoint moving out from it."*

In this formula, a *Seeker's attention* and *presence* are oriented in the first PCL; the last two PCL ("B1" and "B2") would be alternated repeatedly.

It is expected that most of what a *Seeker*

first experiences with this *process* is purely *"imagination"*—meaning that it is *Self-created* in the absence of actual perceptions. Eventually, with practice, a *Seeker* will find that more of their *Awareness* is able to be "established" or "present" in the *secondary viewpoint*.

Recognition of "real perception" with this practice may be subtle at first, but still seem quite real. This is what we would mean by stably *establishing* a *secondary viewpoint* that is "remote" from the *body*. It is *secondary* and *remote* only to the POV that we apply to the *body* and experience with its eyes.

During phases of early progress on the *Pathway*, it is important to acknowledge any personal success or improvement in these areas by simply *ending* the *process*. To continue such practices further without a break may result in some anomaly that causes you to invalidate the gains that were made and feel like all of it was entirely imagined. Consider any "win" as an *end-point*. At the very least, return to it after a break.

Eventually, you would practice this beyond the point of *establishing a viewpoint* in order to continue practicing *"Locational POV"* at a higher-level of application. For example: using a "New Age" suggestion from an "Eastern" technique called *"journeying to other planets,"* we modified the above *process* to include practicing *"Locational POV"* with *any imagined* point in the *Universe.*

A. *"Be near (or above) ---."*

B1. *"Be inside of --- (it)."*

B2. *"Be outside of --- (it)."*

C1. *"Be at the center of --- (it)."*

C2. *"Be outside of --- (it)."*

D1. *"Be on the surface of --- (it)."*

D2. *"Be above --- (it)."*

As an extended process: after a *secondary*

*viewpoint* is established ("A"), each set (e.g. B1 and B2, *&tc.*) are alternated a few times in sequence—working from B to C to D; and then the whole B-C-D cycle is repeated again. Although the *running* of this *process* could be essentially "unlimited," find an appropriate *end-point*.

---

## ADVANCED APPLICATIONS

An entire volume of material—*"Imaginomicon"*—is dedicated to the theory and practice of *"creativeness processing."* The work explored thus far in this lesson falls under that category. These applications have nearly unlimited potential variations. There are many suggestions we can review from that earlier material.

For example, with our original practice of setting up a *secondary viewpoint*: once a *Seeker* has certainty on their ability using a single *alternative POV*, the practice is expanded to include multiple *viewpoints*.

To begin, before considering *additional alternative POV*, a *Seeker* would initially practice by simply alternating between a created *secondary viewpoint* (with eyes closed) and the *POV* of the *body* when eyes are open.

This would mean "*anchoring*" your *alternative POV* above the "mountain" with an intention of "keeping it from going away." Once it is held steady in imagination, a *Seeker* should be able to resume that *viewpoint* (by intention) immediately upon closing their eyes.

Then alternate between viewpoints, spotting something in each: eyes open, *POV-1*; eyes closed, *POV-2*; and so on, until one feels satisfied to end the process.

As an additional gradient of practice, a *Seeker* can increase their *actualized percept-*

*ion* enough to simultaneously *"look"* through both *POV* (with eyes open).

It will be noticed, of course, that the "volume" or "amplitude" of the *perceptions* received from the *body-POV* are considerably "louder" than the *alternative-POV*. To improve on this, even with eyes open, all a *Seeker* has to do is increase the *attention* that is directed to the *alternative-POV* (to keep it from going away).

---

## CREATION-OF-SPACE

The *Alpha-Spirit* has forgotten its own natural ability to *create* and handle *"space."* We have come to rely on the energy-matter of the *Physical Universe* and the sensory perceptions of a *genetic-vehicle* to have any sense of *"space."*

Although the concept of *imagination* and *mental imagery* is treated quite lightly in former instruction, the upper-level consideration is: to truly *create* energy, matter and various forms, there must first be *"space"* *created* for them to exist in. Although difficult to fathom for some readers at first, this is a concept that may actually be practiced in *processing*.

Many mystical practices treat philosophical constructs of *"space"* as "circles" and "spheres." For example: a "magician" *casts* a "circle" to mentally differentiate their own designation of "sacred space" from the surrounding universe. This is an example of dramatizing or mirroring *creation* of a *"Personal Universe."*

Using our methods, we developed a similar exercise that allows a *Seeker* to more *systematically* define the parameters of *created space* by using the philosophical construct of a "cube." A *Seeker* is likely already familiar with the idea of a "cube-like room" to designate a *"space"* as separate from elsewhere. This is far more effective in *processing* than mentally defining the three-dimensional points that compose a "sphere."

Our previous exercises may be extended further for a demonstration of this idea. Rather than use the *facsimile-copy* of a "mountain" as we *re-created* it from something found within this *Universe*, this time we want to actually *imagine* the "mountain" being within the *"space"* of one's own *created* "Personal Universe." This is practiced by:

A. Creating dimensions (defining boundaries) of *"space"*; and then

B. Creating the energetic-masses or forms within that *"space."*

Rather than closing your eyes and essentially *"recalling"* an actual "mountain" from memory in order to duplicate a *facsimile-copy* of the scene, this time we want to *create* fixed dimensions of finite *space* within our *Personal Universe* for which to *imagine* "a mountain" of our own unique design.

Of course, *"Creation-of-Space"* may be practiced cumulatively over the course of multiple *sessions*. It is dependent on a *Seeker's* ability to *imagine (create)* and perceive a single *"point"* with definitive certainty.

This exercise is then extended to include other *"points,"* a *"line"* between two points, a *"square"* composed of four points and four lines, and finally a complete *"cube."* Eventually, a *Seeker* works up to being able to distinctly *perceive* the eight *"points"* to form a *"cube"* of *"space"* within a single *processing* "step" or PCL.

For our technique to be effective, when first starting out: it is far more important to distinctly and fully *create* and *perceive* a single *"point"*—and then even a *"line-segment"* between points, perhaps during a separate *session*—rather than rush progress and only vaguely have certainty on having *created* a stable *"cube."*

Once the "cube" has been sufficiently *imagined*, a *Seeker* may then practice *"intentions,"* such as: *"hold it still," "keep it from going away"* and *"make it more solid,"* to establish greater vividness of the *mental imagery*. [Refer to *Lesson-4* for details regarding use of these PCL in *processing*.]

If it is helpful, these *"intentions"* (*"hold it still," &tc.*) may be applied (as PCL) to each progressive "step" (the *point*, the *line, &tc.*) along the way. Note that it has taken some Seekers a significant amount of practice to simply achieve a total *realization* of *creating* and "holding" even a single point "still" enough to perceive it "solidly."

The original *processing* steps are as follows:

*"Imagine a point."*

*"Imagine a line stretching to a second point."*

*"Imagine lines stretching upwards from those two points to another two points."*

*"Imagine the upper points are connected to form a square."*

*"Imagine another set of four points connected together to form a second square."*

*"Imagine lines connecting the two squares to form a cube."*

*"Imagine that this cube is pure space."*

Once a *Seeker* is skilled in this practice, *processes* (such as "the mountain") that involve *creating* or *imagining* (as opposed to *recalling*) are far more effective when handled within this personally *created* space. For example: rather than closing your eyes and suspending "a mountain" against the background scenery of your mind, you would first *imagine* a large *"cube-of-space"* and *then* the "mountain" within it.

## THE "MUSTS" & "CAN'TS" OF LIFE

Part of the freedom that is recovered in *systematic processing*, is the ability to operate the *Human* "game" without obsessing over "*must haves*" and "*can't haves*" — or the flip-side of this, the "*must avoid*" and "*can't get rid of*" — considerations that seem to so strongly influence our thoughts and actions; or, at the very least, entangle much of our *attentions*.

There are times you may have noticed that when you had *really really* "wanted" something, it tended to remain out of reach; or when you have tried *really* hard to "avoid" something, it seemed to seek you out and practically land on your doorstep. This frustration is a part of the standard-issue *Human Condition*.

By "*must have*" we don't mean, for example, how a "body" *must have* "oxygen."

We mean *intense "desire."* That being said: we aren't implying that you can't really like something and still obtain it, or have it. But, cravings and obsessions are born from *fragmentation.* The more *turbulent, fragmented,* or "desperate" the *attention* or *effort* given by someone, the more difficult it is to "manifest" exactly what they actually want.

Those things which we want (or don't want) are, indeed, *"things,"* which is to say *"terminals."* As such, our experience with them is based on *energy-flows* and *considerations.*

In the case of our usual (and often *fragmented*) participation with *Life*: that which we "reach" *too hard* for will create a "pressure-wave" type *flow* that will actually push the "thing" away; and when we try to "avoid" something *too hard*, we create a "suction-wave" type *flow* that will actually draw the "thing" toward us.

At an upper-level of understanding, attempts to *control* the *flow* using considerations of *"must have"* or *"can't have"* creates an energetic turbulence similar to what we encountered in *Lesson-4* concerning *"Human Problems."* Of course, in that instance (*"problems"*), two basic things in opposition are colliding with each other; here we are specifically considering attracting things we desire and avoiding the undesirable.

There are times when the *clear route* seems *"counter-intuitive"* —but, then we must remember that in most cases our *"intuition"* is likely to also be "clouded" by *fragmentation.* And the real fact is: as we progress on the *Pathway,* our dependency on what some call *"intuition"* is gradually replaced by *true Knowingness.*

True *control* of a "system" often requires only a light touch. In the case of handling *"terminals,"* we are again concerned with one's own level of acceptance. By this we mean *defragmenting* an area (or a *terminal*) to a point where a *Seeker* is *willing* to "have" or "not have" freely. This is the secret key to "*having.*"

By being free of the *fragmentation* related to something, an individual is more likely to "enjoy" it without experiencing the interference of *compulsive obsessions*. In the same wise, *fragmentation* inhibits us from simply walking away from something we are disinterested in, without recoiling in revulsion and disgust.

---

## DEFRAGMENTATION TECHNIQUES

Some of the best *systematic processes* for handling the "*must haves*" of *Life* utilize "*visualization*" or creating "*mental imagery.*" A continuing *Seeker* has had some practice with this already. While some may consider this to be "imaginative-play" only—we are still *systematically processing* our *considerations*. In this case, we use *"mental imagery"* directly to do it, rather than representative words to consider an area.

When we desire or crave a thing intensely, it has a tendency to develop an *automatic consideration* in the "Mind-System." This *consideration* is that the thing has near-infinite value and scarcity or rarity. Such *considerations* conflict with other *reality-agreements* we have about the *"Physical Universe"* when it comes time to encounter or manifest the condition of *having* whatever "it" is.

The systematic solution—although this will seem strange to some readers—is to visualize *"wasting"* (and then eventually *"giving away"*) that which we *want* to *have* so deeply and keep so closely. At first, a *Seeker* might visualize the item being sucked into a vacuum machine or being thrown out into space. Then you can start to *imagine* actually giving it away to others.

This not only increases our fluid "*acceptance*" about the item; it also changes our underlying *perception* or *consideration* of the thing being "so super rare that we probably can't ever have it anyway." Only after this point is reached would an additional step be added of *visualizing* "*receiving*" it from others.

On the other side of this, we have also discussed the idea of obsessively "avoiding" certain undesirable things that seem to always show up in our lives. We have a *fragmented* view of "scarcity" in our lives. The same mechanisms are in play as before, but in reverse. In this case, you would start the previous technique with visualizations about *having more* of an item. The "*giving away*" and "*receiving*" parts remain the same.

These types of *processes* are not meant to

be *run* for excessively long periods; but long enough to feel the "release point" of breaking through a certain "mental barrier" that has been restricting the free-*flow* of energy on the channel (as related to a specific "*terminal*," *&tc*). The *end-point* is not so much of a *realization* as it is a certain "feeling" that some small weight has been "relieved" or has "fallen away."

This technique is not intended to actually "manifest" the condition of actually *having* something; only freeing up the *considerations* about *having* it, which is the required step (often missed) to getting what we want. To get a better sense of how this may be applied to various *terminals*, we'll take up an example.

"*Money*" is a good example to start; it is a general area of concern—and a common area of *turbulent fragmentation*. But, it is a good direct example—because, "*money*" is the equivalent of "*lifeforce energy*" that *flows* in a "human society." It is an integral "system" of "civilization"—and to operate at optimum efficiency, this *energy* must "circulate"; it must *flow*.

Using the above *process*, a *Seeker* would start by *imagining* ways to "*waste money*." It essentially "answers" a PCL for considering what physical actions one might take to "*waste money*," but by *visualizing* various scenes and possible events. *Imagery* should be *created*, not *recalled* from actual memory; and it can be completely ridiculous examples (*e.g.*, "tossing it into a fire"), so long as "*ways to waste money*" is answered.

Once a *Seeker* has worked with this, the additional steps of *processing* may be applied as *circuits*.

1. "*Imagine giving 'money' to someone.*"
2. "*Imagine someone giving 'money' to you.*"
3. "*Imagine someone giving 'money' to others.*"

In many ways, "forms" and "things" are the materialization of a particular "idea" or "concept." In the case of *"money,"* it is really a form of communication exchange that is used in exchange for various goods and services. This, again, makes it a perfect demonstrable example of the next *process.*

A. *"What could 'money' be a substitution for?"*

B. *"What could substitute 'money'?"*

Since one our goals is to freely accept and reject the same "thing" (as an *energy flow*), the following applies to more specific considerations:

A. *"What 'money' could you accept?"*

B. *"What 'money' could you reject?"*

Since we are dealing with a "thing" that we want (or don't want), we treat this type of *processing* differently than just the "concept" of the "thing" alone. If this were purely *"conceptual,"* we would run: *"What 'about money' could you..."* which is a slightly different, but related matter, introduced in previous lessons.

When the more significant turbulence has been quieted down for a particular area, only then is it appropriate to apply other types of *"affirmation"* or *"visualization"* techniques that might directly "attract" a particular energy or *flow* into your life. These are what are more commonly dispensed in typical *"Self-help"* and *"New Age"* material, but without actually handling the underlying *turbulence* or *fragmentation* itself.

As a result, many are turned off by any new "meta-psychological" approach, because the old *"think happy thoughts"* or *"wish it, will it, get it"* or *"help me, help you, help me, sell more pop-Self-help books"* didn't produce the stable results promised. A few people may have been the richer for it; mainly the authors. *Systemol-*

*ogy* is not intended to be viewed in this same light. Our results speak for themselves with each individual *Seeker*.

To experiment with our philosophy further, using a *"New Thought"* exercise (in the direction of "fluidity" and "attraction"), try the following visualization exercise with your eyes closed.

*Imagine* "clouds" of "money" around your body. Then using *intention*, "push" those "clouds" into the body. Be careful not to "pull" them from the "inside" as this only reinforces the sensation of *Beingness* as a body. After doing this several times, *Imagine* these "clouds" and use *intention* to "throw them away" or else "explode" off in the distance. Then alternate back to *imagining* and *"pushing them in."*

If either of these *"flows"* seems more difficult—or suddenly becomes more difficult—then concentrate on doing the "other" a few more times before alternating.

In the beginning of the exercise, it is easier to *imagine* handling "smaller" or "lower-grade" versions of the item (*"money"*) and then gradually improve the "value" represented (for example, "copper" into "silver" into "gold" *&tc*).

After you have worked through this material concerning *"money,"* consider applying the full cycle of *processing* given in this *"defragmentation"* section of the lesson to various things like: "FOOD," "SEX," and "JOBS" (or "WORK") for additional practice.

Eventually, a *Seeker* will want to *run* this on the actual (specific) stuff they *"really really want"* (and perhaps haven't been able to get, or blatantly *"can't have"*). The *"desires"* that run strong with an individual will be uniquely specific to them and cannot be covered fully here; but the same *procedure* given above is applied.

## "AVOIDING" & "GETTING RID OF"

Having treated the area of *"wants," "must haves"* and *"can't haves"* above, the next step is to consider the other side of this: that which a *Seeker* feels they *"must avoid"* in *Life*, but can't seem to *"get rid of."*

Although we are treating all of these areas with words, at an upper-level, we are really handling the *energy-flows* of *attention*—and the *energetic-masses* that these form when *flowing* in one-direction too long. We can become so concentrated and fixed upon something that our *attention-energy* actually builds up a "pressure-like force" or "mass" that continues to press against something *oppositional* or *blocking*.

For example: when we were treating the area of *"must have,"* we began our *processing* by *knowingly* reversing the "stuck" (or *compulsively* "one-way") *flow* regarding the *terminal*, and "*wasting*" it, or "*throwing it away*." Once the *turbulent fragmentation* is handled, the "*acceptance-and-rejection*" type of *processing* simply provides greater stability (or certainty) for handling that *flow fluidly*.

In order to *systematically process* an *attention-flow* regarding the opposite—something that won't go away, or that a person is trying to be rid of (or avoid)—the first PCL of the previous *procedure* would be opposite. This means reversing the *flow* by *imagining* ways of "*having more*" rather than "*wasting*." The remainder of the *processing*—concerning "*giving-and-receiving*" and "*acceptance-and-rejection*" is identical.

For the previous demonstration, we used "*money*" as a common general example of something *desirous* to *have*. For this opposite demonstration, we will also use something general and common that most lifeforms dislike strongly and try to avoid: *pain.*

Usually this "reflexive" or "compulsive" use of our *attention* will cause us to attract more of what we are obsessively trying to avoid and/or to experience it more vividly when it does occur.

As a quick rundown of procedure, the first PCL (of the first *process*) is: "*Imagine ways to have more pain.*" The remainder of the *process* consists of: "*Imagine ways to give 'pain' away*" and "*Imagine ways to receive pain.*"

It is important, again, to *create* and not to "*recall*" actual events for this type of *processing.* Once a *Seeker* has *run* this, the *processing* may be applied directly as *circuits* as given here:

1. "*Imagine giving 'pain' to someone.*"
2. "*Imagine someone giving 'pain' to you.*"
3. "*Imagine someone giving 'pain' to others.*"

And for the considerations:

A. *"What could 'pain' be a substitution for?"*
B. *"What could substitute 'pain'?"*

And finally:

A. *"What 'pain' could you accept?"*
B. *"What 'pain' could you reject?"*

If you were to apply the final *"visualization exercise"* from the original *procedure* above, than you would *imagine* "clouds" of "pain" around you—alternating the *"push in"* on the body and the *"throw away"* steps. As an extension of the *procedure* (for both sides), a *Seeker* can then *imagine* the representation of it and alternate *running* concepts of "connection" and "separation" (or disconnection).

A. *"Get the sense of being connected to it."*
B. *"Get the sense of being separate from it."*

This is *run* until a *Seeker* no longer feels

any *compulsive* °*creation* of a one-way "stuck" *flow*; which is to say, there is no longer a *flinch*, *craving* or *reactive-response* regarding that "channel" (to a particular *terminal*). Again, this regimen runs into areas that will apply uniquely and specifically for each individual, so the best we can provide in this *Professional Course* is a series of *processes* that have the widest possible *application*.

*The Systemology Professional Course*
continues in the next lesson booklet:
**ESCAPING SPIRIT-TRAPS**

# GLOSSARY

**actualization** : to make actual, not just potential; to bring into full solid Reality; to realize fully in *Awareness* as a "thing."

**agreement (reality)** : unanimity of opinion of what is "thought" to be known; an accepted arrangement of how things are; things we consider as "real" or as an "is" of "reality"; a consensus of what is real as made by standard-issue (common) participants; what an individual contributes to or accepts as "real"; in *Systemology*, a synonym for *"reality."*

**alpha** : the first, primary, basic, superior or beginning of some form; in *Systemology*, referring to the state of existence operating on spiritual archetypes and postulates, will and intention "exterior" to the low-level condensation and solidarity of energy and matter as the 'physical universe' (*beta*).

**alpha-spirit** : a "spiritual" *Life*-form; the "true" *Self* or I-AM; the *individual*; the spiritual (*alpha*) *Self* that is animating the (*beta*) physical body or *"genetic vehicle"* using a continuous *Lifeline* of spiritual (*"ZU"*) energy; an individu-

74

al spiritual (*alpha*) entity possessing no physical mass or measurable waveform (motion) in the Physical Universe as itself, so it animates the (*beta*) physical body or "*genetic vehicle*" as a catalyst to experience *Self*-determined causality in effect within the *Physical Universe*; a singular unit or point of *Spiritual Awareness* that is *Aware* that it is *Aware*.

**alpha thought** : the highest spiritual *Self-determination* over creation and existence exercised by an Alpha-Spirit; the Alpha range of pure *Creative Ability* based on direct postulates and considerations of *Beingness*; spiritual qualities comparable to "thought" but originating in Alpha-existence, independently superior to a Mind-System.

**ascension** : actualized *Awareness* elevated to the point of true "spiritual existence" exterior to *beta existence*. An "Ascended Master" is one who has returned to an incarnation on Earth as an inherently *Enlightened One*, demonstrable in their words and actions; they have the ability to *Self-direct* the "Mind" and "Body" as *Self* (as a "Spirit"); and to maintain consciousness as a personal identity continuum with the same *Self-directed* control and communication of Will-Intention that is exercised, actualized and developed deliberately during one's present incarnation.

**associative knowledge** : significance or meaning of a facet or aspect assigned to (or considered to have) a direct relationship with another facet; to connect or relate ideas or facets of existence with one another; in traditional systems logic, an equivalency of significance or meaning between facets or sets that are grouped together, such as in *(a + b) + c = a + (b + c)*; in Systemology, erroneous associative knowledge is assignment of the same value to all facets or parts considered as related (even when they are not actually so), such as in *a = a, b = a, c = a* and so forth without distinction.

**attention** : active use of *Awareness* toward a specific aspect or thing; the act of "attending" with the presence of *Self*; a direction of focus or concentration of *Awareness* along a particular channel or conduit or toward a particular terminal node or communication termination point; the Self-directed concentration of personal energy as a combination of observation, thought-waves and consideration; focused application of *Self-Directed Awareness*.

**awareness** : the highest sense of-and-as *Self* in knowing and being as I-AM (the *Alpha-Spirit*); the extent of beingness directed as a viewpoint (POV) experienced by *Self* as knowingness.

**beta (existence)** : all manifestation in the "Physical Universe" (KI, in *Zuism*); the conditions of *Awareness* for the *Alpha-spirit* (*Self*) as a physical organic *Lifeform* or "*genetic vehicle*" in which it experiences causality in the *Physical Universe*.

**charge** : to fill or furnish with a quality; to supply with energy; to lay a command upon; in *Systemology*—to imbue with intention; to overspread with emotion; personal energy stores and significances entwined as fragmentation in mental images, reactive-response encoding and intellectual (and/or) programmed beliefs.

**circuit** : a circular path or loop; a closed-path within a system that allows a flow; a pattern or action or wave movement that follows a specific route or potential path only; in *Systemology*, "*communication processing*" pertaining to a specific *flow* of energy or information along a channel; "*feedback loop.*"

**communication** : successful transmission of information, data, energy (&tc.) along a message line, with a reception of feedback; an energetic flow of intention to cause an effect (or duplication) at a distance; the personal energy moved or acted upon by will or else 'selective directed attention'; the 'messenger action' used to transmit and receive energy across a medium; also relay of energy, a message or signal—or even locating a personal POV (viewpoint) for the Self—along the *ZU-line*.

**confront** : to come around in front of; to be in the presence of; to stand in front of, or in the face of; to meet "face-to-face" or "face-up-to"; additionally, in *Systemology*, to fully tolerate or acceptably withstand an encounter with a particular manifestation or encounter.

**defragmentation** : the *reparation* of wholeness; collecting all dispersed parts to reform an original whole; a process of removing "*fragmentation*" in data or knowledge to provide a clear understanding; applying techniques and processes that promote a *holistic* interconnected *alpha* state, favoring observational *Awareness* of continuity in all spiritual and physical systems; in *Systemology*, a "*Seeker*" achieving actualized "*Self-Honest Awareness*" is said to be in a basic state of *beta-defragmentation*, whereas *Alpha-defragmentation* is the rehabilitation of the *creative ability*, managing the *Spiritual Timeline* and the POV of *Self* as Alpha-Spirit (I-AM).

**fragmentation** : breaking into parts and scattering the pieces; the *fractioning* of wholeness or the *fracture* of a holistic interconnected *alpha* state, favoring observational *Awareness* of perceived connectivity between parts; *discontinuity*; separation of a totality into parts; in *Systemology*, a person outside of *Self-Honesty* is said to be operating from a *fragmented* state.

**flow** : movement across (or through) a channel (or conduit); a direction of active energetic motion, typically distinguished as either an *in-flow*, *out-flow* or *cross-flow*.

**genetic-vehicle** : a physical *Life*-form; the physical (*beta*) body that is animated/controlled by the (*Alpha*) *Spirit* using a continuous *Spiritual Lifeline* (ZU); a physical (*beta*) organic receptacle and catalyst for the (*Alpha*) *Self* to operate "causes" and experience "effects" within the *Physical Universe*.

**holistic** : the examination of interconnected systems as encompassing something greater than the *sum* of their "parts."

**Human Condition** : a standard default state of Human experience that is generally accepted to be the extent of its potential identity (*beingness*) —currently treated as *Homo Sapiens Sapiens,* but which is scheduled for replacement by *Homo Novus* (the "New Human").

**imprint** : to strongly impress, stamp, mark (or outline) onto a softer 'impressible' substance; to mark with pressure onto a surface; in *Systemology*, used to indicate permanent Reality impressions marked by frequencies, energies or interactions experienced during periods of emotional distress, pain, unconsciousness, loss, enforcement, or something antagonistic to physical (personal) survival, all of which are are stored with other reactive response-mechanisms at lower-levels of *Awareness* as opposed to the active memory database and proactive processing center of the Mind; an experiential "memory-set" that may later resurface—be triggered or stimulated artificially—as Reality, of which similar responses will be engaged automatically; holographic-like imagery "stamped" onto consciousness as composed of energetic *facets* tied to the "snap-shot" of an experience.

**pilot** : a professional steersman responsible for healthy functional operation of a ship toward a specific destination; in *Systemology*, an intensive trained individual qualified to specially apply *Systemology Processing* to assist other *Seekers* on the *Pathway*.

**point-of-view (POV)** : a point to view from; an opinion or attitude as expressed from a specific identity-phase; a specific standpoint or vantage-point; a definitive manner of consideration specific to an individual phase or identity; a place or position affording a specific view or vantage; circumstances and programming of an individual that is conducive to a particular response, consideration or belief-set (paradigm); a position (consideration) or place (location) that provides a specific view or perspective (subjective) on experience (of the objective).

**postulate** : to put forward as truth; to suggest or assume an existence *to be*; to state or affirm the existence of particular conditions; to provide a basis of reasoning and belief; a basic theory accepted as fact; in *NexGen Systemology*, "Alpha-Thought"—the top-most decisions or considerations made by the Alpha-Spirit regarding the "*is-ness*" (what things "are") about energy-matter and space-time.

**presence** : a quality of some thing (*energy/matter*) being "present" in space-time; personal orientation of *Self* as an *Awareness* (*POV*) located in present space-time (environment) and communicating with extant energy-matter.

**processing command line (PCL)** or **command line** : a directed input; a specific command using highly selective language for *Systemology Processing*; a predetermined directive statement (cause) intended to focus concentrated attention (effect).

**processing, systematic** : the inner-workings or "through-put" result of systems; in *Systemology*, a method of applied spiritual technology used toward personal Self-Actualization; methods of selective directed attention, communicated language and associative imagery that increases personal control of the human condition.

**realization** : the clear perception of an understanding; a consideration or understanding on what is "actual"; to make "real" or give "reality" to so as to grant a property of "beingness" or "being as it is"; the state or instance of coming to an *Awareness*; in *Systemology*, "gnosis" or true knowledge achieved during *systematic processing*; achievement of a new (or "higher") cognition, true knowledge or perception of Self; a consideration of reality or assignment of meaning.

**responsibility** : the *ability* to *respond*; the extent of mobilizing *power* and *understanding* an individual maintains as *Awareness* to enact *change*; the proactive ability to *Self-direct* and make decisions independent of an outside authority.

**Seeker** : an individual on the *Pathway to Self-Honesty*; a practitioner of *Mardukite Systemology* or *Systemology Processing*, that is working toward *Spiritual Ascension*.

**Self-actualization** : bringing the full potential of the Human spirit into Reality; expressing full capabilities and creativeness of the *Alpha-Spirit*.

**Self-determinism** : the freedom to act, clear of external control or influence; the personal control of Will to direct intention.

**Self-honesty** : the basic or original *alpha* state of *being* and *knowing*; clear and present total *Awareness* of-and-as *Self*, in its most basic and true proactive expression of itself as *Spirit* or *I-AM*—free of artificial attachments, perceptive filters and other emotionally-reactive or mentally-conditioned programming imposed on the human condition by the systematized physical world; the ability to experience existence without judgment.

**spiritual timeline** : a continuous stream of moment-to-moment *Mental Images* (or a record of experiences) that defines the "past" of a spiritual being (or *Alpha-Spirit*) and which includes impressions (*imprints, &tc.*) from all life-incarnations and significant spiritual events the being has encountered; in Systemology, also "*backtrack*."

**Systemology** : a modern tradition of applied religious philosophy and spiritual technology based on *Arcane Tablets* (in combination with

"*general systemology*" and "*games theory*") developed in the New Age underground by Joshua
Free in 2011 as an advanced futurist extension
of the *Mardukite Research Org.*; also known as
"*Mardukite Systemology,*" "*Metahuman Systemology*" and "*Spiritual Systemology.*"

**terminal (node)** : a point, end, or mass, on a
line; a connection point for closing an electric
circuit, such as a post on a battery terminating
at each end of its own systematic function; a
point of connectivity with other points; in systems, a contact point of interaction; a point of
interaction with other points.

**turbulence** : a quality or state of distortion or
disturbance that creates irregularity of a flow or
pattern; the quality or state of aberration on a
line (such as ragged edges) or the emotional
"turbulent feelings" attached to a particular flow
or terminal node; a violent, haphazard or dishar-
monious commotion (such as in the ebb of gusts
and lulls of wind action).

**willingness** : the state of conscious Self-determined ability and interest (directed attention)
to *Be*, *Do* or *Have*; a Self-determined consideration to reach, face up to (*confront*) or manage
some "mass" or energy; the extent to which an
individual considers themselves able to particip-
ate, act or communicate along some line, to put

attention or intention on the line, or to produce (create) an effect.

*ZU* : the ancient Sumerian cuneiform sign for the archaic verb—"*to know*," "*knowingness*" or "*awareness*"; in *Mardukite Zuism and Systemology*, the active energy/matter of the "Spiritual Universe" (AN) experienced as a *Lifeforce* or *consciousness* that imbues living forms extant in the "Physical Universe" (KI); "*Spiritual Life Energy*"; energy demonstrated by the WILL of an actualized *Alpha-Spirit* in the "Spiritual Universe" (AN), which impinges its *Awareness* into the Physical Universe (KI), animating/controlling *Life* for its experience of *beta-existence* along an individual Alpha-Spirit's personal *Identity-continuum*, called a *ZU-line*.

**Zu-Line** : a theoretical construct in *Mardukite Zuism and Systemology* demonstrating *Spiritual Life Energy* (*ZU*) as a personal individual "continuum" of Awareness interacting with all Spheres of Existence on the Standard Model of Systemology; a spectrum of potential variations and interactions of a monistic continuum or singular *Spiritual Life Energy (ZU)* demonstrated on the Standard Model; an energetic channel of potential POV and "locations" of Beingness, demonstrated in early Systemology materials as an individual Alpha-Spirit's personal *Identity-*

*continuum*, potentially connecting *Awareness (ZU)* of *Self* with *"Infinity"* simultaneous with all points considered in existence; a symbolic demonstration of the *"Life-line"* on which *Awareness (ZU)* extends from the direction of the "Spiritual Universe" (AN) in its true original *alpha state* through an entire possible range of activity resulting in its *beta state* and control of a *genetic-entity* occupying the *Physical Universe (KI)*.

**Zu-Vision** : the true and basic (*Alpha*) Point-of-View (perspective, POV) maintained by *Self* as *Alpha-Spirit* outside boundaries or considerations of the *Human Condition* "Mind-Systems" and *exterior* to beta-existence reality agreements with the Physical Universe; a POV of Self *as* "a unit of Spiritual Awareness" that exists independent of a "body" and entrapment in a *Human Condition*; "spirit vision" in its truest sense.

# Fundamentals of Systemology
*in six*
Basic Course Lesson Booklets

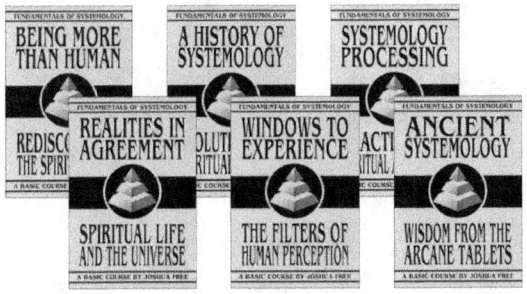

<table>
<tr><td>BEING MORE<br>THAN HUMAN</td><td>A HISTORY OF<br>SYSTEMOLOGY</td><td>SYSTEMOLOGY<br>PROCESSING</td></tr>
<tr><td>REDISC(<br>THE SPIRI</td><td>REALITIES IN<br>AGREEMENT</td><td>WINDOWS TO<br>EXPERIENCE</td><td>ANCIENT<br>SYSTEMOLOGY</td></tr>
<tr><td>SPIRITUAL LIFE<br>AND THE UNIVERSE</td><td>THE FILTERS OF<br>HUMAN PERCEPTION</td><td>WISDOM FROM THE<br>ARCANE TABLETS</td></tr>
</table>

Also
available
as a
*six-in-one*
hardcover
edition!

# THE SYSTEMOL

Seekers and students of the *Basic Course* and *Professional Course* will also be interested in the *Advanced Series* of the *Systemology Core*. These volumes are a complete chronological record of the Mardukite New Thought developments from the Systemology Society, published in 2019 through 2023.

The *Systemology Core* begins with the first professional publication released when the *Mardukite Systemology Society* emerged from the underground in 2019, with: *"The Tablets of Destiny Revelation."*

# OGY PATHWAY

PUBLISHED BY THE **JOSHUA FREE** IMPRINT REPRESENTING

**The Mardukite Academy of Systemology**

THE JOSHUA FREE IMPRINT
JFI PUBLICATIONS

MARDUKITE
ZUISM

**mardukite.com**

www.ingramcontent.com/pod-product-compliance
Lightning Source LLC
Chambersburg PA
CBHW071213120626
46546CB00006B/2546